D1126342

New & Selected Poems

DONALD DAVIE

New &
Selected
Poems

Wesleyan University Press
MIDDLETOWN, CONNECTICUT

For Doreen:

who else?

Contents

New & Selected Poems

Woodpigeons at Raheny

One simple and effective rhyme
Over and over in the April light;
   And a touch of the old time
In the serving-man stooping, aproned tight,
At the end of the dappled avenue
To the easy phrase, "tereu-tereu",
Mulled over by the sleepy dove—
This was the poem I had to write.

White wall where the creepers climb
Year after year on the sunny side;
   And a touch of the old time
In the sandalled Capuchin's silent stride
Over the shadows and through the clear
Cushion-soft wooing of the ear
From two meadows away, by the dove—
This was the poem that was denied.

For whether it was the friar's crime,
His lean-ness suddenly out of tune;
   Or a touch of the old time
In the given phrase, with its unsought boon
Of a lax autumnal atmosphere,
Seemed quaint and out of keeping here,
I do not know. I know the dove
Outsang me down the afternoon.

On Bertrand Russell's "Portraits from Memory"

Those Cambridge generations, Russell's, Keynes' . . .
And mine? Oh mine was Wittgenstein's, no doubt;
Sweet pastoral, too, when some one else explains,
Although my memories leave the eclogues out.

The clod's not bowed by sedentary years
Yet, set by Thyrsis, he's a crippled man:
How singularly naked each appears,
Beside the other on this bosky plan.

Arrangements of the copse and cloister seem,
Although effective, still Utopian,
For groves find room, behind a leafy screen,
For sage and harvester, but not for man.

I wonder still which of the hemispheres
Infects the other, in this grassy globe;
The chumbling moth of Madingley, that blears
The labourer's lamp, destroys the scarlet robe.

It was the Muse that could not make her home
In that too thin and yet too sluggish air,
Too volatile to live among the loam,
Her sheaves too heavy for the talkers there.

Creon's Mouse

Creon, I think, could never kill a mouse
When once that dangerous girl was put away,
Shut up unbridled in her rocky house,
Colossal nerve denied the light of day.

Now Europe's hero, the humaner King
Who hates himself, is humanized by shame,
Is he a curbed or a corroded spring?
A will that's bent, or buckled? Tense, or tame?

If too much daring brought (he thought) the war,
When that was over nothing else would serve
But no one must be daring any more,
A self-induced and stubborn loss of nerve.

In itching wainscot having met his match,
He waits unnerved, and hears his caverned doom,
The nausea that struggles to dispatch
Pink-handed horror in a craggy room.

The absolute endeavour was the catch;
To clean the means and never mind the end
Meant he had not to chasten but to scotch
The will he might have managed to amend.

You that may think yourselves not proud at all,
Learn this at least from humble Creon's fall:
The will that is subjèct, not overthrown,
Is humbled by some power not its own.

Remembering the Thirties

Hearing one saga, we enact the next.
We please our elders when we sit enthralled;
But then they're puzzled; and at last they're vexed
To have their youth so avidly recalled.

It dawns upon the veterans after all
That what for them were agonies, for us
Are highbrow thrillers, though historical;
And all their feats quite strictly fabulous.

This novel written fifteen years ago,
Set in my boyhood and my boyhood home,
These poems about "abandoned workings" show
Worlds more remote than Ithaca or Rome.

The Anschluss, Guernica—all the names
At which those poets thrilled or were afraid
For me mean schools and schoolmasters and games;
And in the process some one is betrayed.

Ourselves perhaps. The Devil for a joke
Might carve his own initials on our desk,
And yet we'd miss the point because he spoke
An idiom too dated, Audenesque.

Ralegh's Guiana also killed his son.
A pretty pickle if we came to see
The tallest story really packed a gun,
The Telemachiad an Odyssey.

Even to them the tales were not so true
As not to be ridiculous as well:
The ironmaster met his Waterloo,
But Rider Haggard rode along the fell.

"Leave for Cape Wrath tonight!" They lounged away
On Fleming's trek or Isherwood's ascent.
England expected every man that day
To show his motives were ambivalent.

They played the fool, not to appear as fools
In time's long glass. A deprecating air
Disarmed, they thought, the jeers of later schools;
Yet irony itself is doctrinaire,

And, curiously, nothing now betrays
Their type to time's derision like this coy
Insistence on the quizzical, their craze
For showing Hector was a mother's boy.

A neutral tone is nowadays preferred.
And yet it may be better, if we must,
To find the stance impressive and absurd
Than not to see the hero for the dust.

For courage is the vegetable king,
The sprig of all ontologies, the weed
That beards the slag-heap with his hectoring,
Whose green adventure is to run to seed.

Hypochondriac Logic

Appendicitis is his worst
Obsession, mordant from the first
And unannounced. For who but he,
By curious failing schooled to see
The tiniest pain, can hope to be
Forewarned of appendectomy?
So thinking, he thinks pain to be
More real as more illusory.

So argue all men who have thought
A truth more true as more remote,
Or in poetic worlds confide
The more their air is rarefied.
This the Shelleyan failing is,
Who feared elephantiasis,
Whose poems infect his readers too,
Who, since they're vague, suppose them true.

But lagging down a crippled street
Like fugitives from their own feet,
Some who are whole can yet observe
Disease is what we all deserve,
Or else disdain a painless life
While any squeal beneath the knife.
So, if you trace the impulse back,
The best are hypochondriac.

So poets may astonish you
With what is not, but should be, true,
And shackle on a moral shape
You only thought you could escape;
So if their scenery is queer,

Its prototype may not be here,
Unless inside a frightened mind,
Which may be dazzled, but not blind.

Heart Beats

If music be the muses' paragon,
Where mostly pure relation is expressed,
The poet looks accusingly upon
This cramped performer drumming in his breast.

"Why brag," he cries, "of buffetings survived
To make the high-pitched harmonies of strain?
You suffer, but some colder thing contrived,
Articulated, and endorsed the pain."

As from a cellar, unrepentant comes
The virtuoso's lunatic tattoo,
Beating to parley in a school of drums:
"I plot the passions, and endure them too."

The Evangelist

"My brethren . . ." And a bland, elastic smile
Basks on the mobile features of Dissent.
No hypocrite, you understand. The style
Befits a church that's based on sentiment.

Solicitations of a swirling gown,
The sudden vox humana, and the pause,
The expert orchestration of a frown
Deserve, no doubt, a murmur of applause.

The tides of feeling round me rise and sink;
Bunyan, however, found a place for wit.
Yes, I am more persuaded than I think;
Which is, perhaps, why I disparage it.

You round upon me, generously keen:
The man, you say, is patently sincere.
Because he is so eloquent, you mean?
That test was never patented, my dear.

If, when he plays upon our sympathies,
I'm pleased to be fastidious, and you
To be inspired, the vice in it is this:
Each does us credit, and we know it too.

A Winter Talent

Lighting a spill late in the afternoon,
I am that coal whose heat it should unfix;
Winter is come again, and none too soon
For meditation on its raft of sticks.

Some quick bright talents can dispense with coals
And burn their boats continually, command
An unreflecting brightness that unrolls
Out of whatever firings come to hand.

What though less sunny spirits never turn
The dry detritus of an August hill
To dangerous glory? Better still to burn
Upon that gloom where all have felt a chill.

The Wind at Penistone

The wind meets me at Penistone.
                            A hill
Curves empty through the township, on a slope
Not cruel, and yet steep enough to be,
Were it protracted, cruel.
                            In the street,
A plain-ness rather meagre than severe,
Affords, though quite unclassical, a vista
So bald as to be monumental.
                            Here
A lean young housewife meets me with the glance
I like to think that I can recognize
As dour, not cross.
                            And all the while the wind,
A royal catspaw, toying easily,
Flicks out of shadows from a tufted wrist,
Its mane, perhaps, this lemon-coloured sun.

The wind reserves, the hill reserves, the style
Of building houses on the hill reserves
A latent edge;
                            which we can do without
In Pennine gradients and the Pennine wind,
And never miss or, missing it, applaud
The absence of the aquiline;
                            which in her
Whose style of living in the wind reserves
An edge to meet the wind's edge, we may miss
But without prejudice.
                            And yet in art
Where all is patent, and a latency

Is manifest or nothing, even I,
Liking to think I feel these sympathies,
Can hardly praise this clenched and muffled style.

For architecture asks a cleaner edge,
Is open-handed.
                    And close-fisted people
Are mostly vulgar; only in the best,
Who draw, inflexible, upon reserves,
Is there a stern game that they play with life,
In which the rule is not to show one's hand
Until compelled.
                    And then the lion's paw!
Art that is dour and leonine in the Alps
Grows kittenish, makes curios and clocks,
Giant at play.
                    Here, nothing. So the wind
Meets me at Penistone, and, coming home,
The poet falls to special pleading, chilled
To find in Art no fellow but the wind.

Samuel Beckett's Dublin

When it is cold it stinks, and not till then.
The seasonable or more rabid heats
Of love and summer in some other cities
Unseal the all too human: not in his.
When it is cold it stinks, but not before;

Smells to high heaven then most creaturely
When it is cold. It stinks, but not before
His freezing eye has done its best to maim,
To amputate limbs, livelihood and name,
Abstracting life beyond all likelihood.

When it is cold it stinks, and not till then
Can it be fragrant. On canal and street,
Colder and colder, Murphy to Molloy,
The weather hardens round the Idiot Boy,
The gleeful hero of the long retreat.

When he is cold he stinks, but not before,
This living corpse. The existential weather
Smells out in these abortive minims, men
Who barely living therefore altogether
Live till they die; and sweetly smell till then.

Time Passing, Beloved

Time passing, and the memories of love
Coming back to me, carissima, no more mockingly
Than ever before; time passing, unslackening,
Unhastening, steadily; and no more
Bitterly, beloved, the memories of love
Coming into the shore.

How will it end? Time passing, and our passages of love
As ever, beloved, blind
As ever before; time binding, unbinding
About us; and yet to remember
Never less chastening, nor the flame of love
Less like an ember.

What will become of us? Time
Passing, beloved, and we in a sealed
Assurance unassailed
By memory. How can it end,
This siege of a shore that no misgivings have steeled,
No doubts defend?

Obiter Dicta

Trying to understand myself, I fetch
    My father's image to me. There he is, augmenting
    The treasury of his prudence with a clutch
Of those cold eggs, Great Truths—his scrivener's hand
    Confiding apothegms to his pocket book.
    Does mine do more than snap the elastic band
Of rhyme about them? In an age that teaches
    How pearls of wisdom only look like eggs,
    The tide, afflatus, still piles up on the beaches
Pearls that he prizes, stones that he retrieves
    Misguidedly from poetry's undertow,
    Deaf to the harsh retraction that achieves
Its scuttering backwash, ironies. And yet,
    Recalling his garrulity, I see
    There's method in it. Seeming to forget
The point at issue, the palmer tells his beads,
    Strung by connections nonchalantly weak
    Upon the thread of argument he needs
To bring them through his fingers, round and round,
    Tasting of gristle, savoury; and he hears,
    Like rubbing stones, their dry conclusive sound.

Himself an actor (he can play the clown),
    He knows the poet's a man of parts; the sage
Is one of them, buffoonery like his own,
    Means to an end. So, if he loves the page
That grows sententious with a terse distinction,
    Yet lapidary moralists are dumb
About the precepts that he acts upon,
    Brown with tobacco from his rule of thumb.

"Not bread but a stone!"—the deep-sea fishermen

Denounce our findings, father. Pebbles, beads,
   Perspicuous dicta, gems from Emerson,
Whatever stands when all about it slides,
   Whatever in the oceanic welter
   Puts period to unpunctuated tides,
These, that we like, they hate. And after all, for you,
   To take but with a pinch of salt to take
   The maxims of the sages is the true
Great Truth of all. To keep, as you would say,
   A sense of proportion, I should portion out
   The archipelago across the bay,
One island to so much sea. Assorted
   Poetic pleasures come in bundles then,
   Strapped up by rhyme, not otherwise supported?

Turning about his various gems to take
   Each other's lustre by a temperate rule,
He walks the graveyard where I have to make
   Not centos but inscriptions, and a whole
That's moved from inward, dancing. Yet I trace
   Among his shored-up epitaphs my own:
Art, as he hints, turns on a commonplace,
   And Death is a tune to dance to, cut in stone.

The Mushroom Gatherers

After Mickiewicz

Strange walkers! See their processional
Perambulations under low boughs,
The birches white, and the green turf under.
These should be ghosts by moonlight wandering.

Their attitudes strange; the human tree
Slowly revolves on its bole. All around
Downcast looks; and the direct dreamer
Treads out in trance his lane, unwavering.

Strange decorum: so prodigal of bows,
Yet lost in thought and self-absorbed, they meet
Impassively, without acknowledgment.
A courteous nation, but unsociable.

Field full of folk, in their immunity
From human ills, crestfallen and serene,
Who would have thought these shades our lively friends?
Surely these acres are Elysian Fields.

The Fountain

Feathers up fast, and steeples; then in clods
Thuds into its first basin; thence as surf
Smokes up and hangs; irregularly slops
Into its second, tattered like a shawl;
There, chill as rain, stipples a danker green,
Where urgent tritons lob their heavy jets.

For Berkeley this was human thought, that mounts
From bland assumptions to inquiring skies,
There glints with wit, fumes into fancies, plays
With its negations, and at last descends,
As by a law of nature to its bowl
Of thus enlightened but still common sense.

We who have no such confidence must gaze
With all the more affection on these forms,
These spires, these plumes, these calm reflections, these
Similitudes of surf and turf and shawl,
Graceful returns upon acceptances.
We ask of fountains only that they play,

Though that was not what Berkeley meant at all.

Cherry Ripe

On a Painting by Juan Gris

No ripening curve can be allowed to sag
On cubist's canvas or in sculptor's stone:
Informal fruit, that burgeons from the swag,
Would spoil the ripening that is art's alone.

This can be done with cherries. Other fruit
Have too much bloom of import, like the grape,
Whose opulence comes welling from a root
Struck far too deep to yield so pure a shape.

And Cherry ripe, indeed ripe, ripe, I cry;
Let orchards flourish in the poet's soul
And bear their feelings that are mastered by
Maturing rhythms, to compose a whole.

But how the shameful grapes and olives swell,
Excrescent from no cornucopia, tart,
Too near to oozing to be handled well:
Ripe, ripe, they cry, and perish in my heart.

Hearing Russian Spoken

Unsettled again and hearing Russian spoken
I think of brokenness perversely planned
By Dostoievsky's debauchees; recall
The "visible brokenness" that is the token
Of the true believer; and connect it all
With speaking a language I cannot command.

If broken means unmusical I speak
Even in English brokenly, a man
Wretched enough, yet one who cannot borrow
Their hunger for indignity nor, weak,
Abet my weakness, drink to drown a sorrow
Or write in metres that I cannot scan.

Unsettled again at hearing Russian spoken,
"Abjure politic brokenness for good",
I tell myself. "Recall what menaces,
What self-loathings must be re-awoken:
This girl and that, and all your promises
Your pidgin that they too well understood."

Not just in Russian but in any tongue
Abandonment, morality's soubrette
Of lyrical surrender and excess,
Knows the weak endings equal to the strong;
She trades on broken English with success
And, disenchanted, I'm enamoured yet.

Under St. Paul's

Wren and Barry, Rennie and Mylne and Dance
    Under the flags the men who stood for stone
    Lie in the stone. Carillons, pigeons once
Sluiced Ludgate's issues daily, and the dome
    Of stone-revetted crystal swung and hung
    Its wealth of waters. Wren had plugged it home
With a crypt at the nerve of London. Now the gull
    Circles the dry stone nozzles of the belfries,
    Each graceful City hydrant of the full
Eagerly brimming measure of agreement,
    Still to be tapped by any well-disposed
    Conversible man, still underneath the pavement
Purling and running, affable and in earnest,
    The conduit, Candour. Fattily urbane
    Under the great drum, pigeons foul their nest.

The whiter wing, Anger, and the gull's
Shearwater raucous over hunting hulls
Seek London's river. Rivers underground,
Under the crypt, return the sound
Of footfalls in the evening city. Wells,
Churchyards sunk behind Fleet Street, utter smells
Of water where a calm conviction spoke
Now dank and standing. Leaves and our debris choke
The bell-note Candour that the paviour heard
Fluting and swelling like a crop-filled bird.

Suppose those tides, from under a masonry shelf
    With great white blind fish, float into sunlight
    From a dark behind Candour, darkness of love itself;
Conviction's claim still holds us, to deny
    Nothing that's undeniable. Light airs

Are bent to the birds that couple as they fly
And slide and soar, yet answer to the flow
　　Of this broad water under. There we ride
　　Lent to the current, and convictions grow
In those they are meant for. As Conviction's face
　　Is darker than the speculative air,
　　So and no darker is the place
For Candour and Love. Do fowls live underwater,
　　Breed in that dark? And hadn't a contriver
　　Of alphabets, Cadmus, the gull for daughter?

Across the dark face of the waters
Flies the white bird, and the waters
Mount, mount, or should mount. We grow surer
Of what we know, if no surer
Of what we think. For on failing,
Labouring now and subsiding and nerveless wing,
The gull sips the body of water. And the air,
Packed at that level, can hold up a minster in air.
Across the dark face of the water
Flies the white bird until nothing is left but the water.

North Dublin

St. George's, Hardwicke Street,
Is charming in the Church of Ireland fashion:
The best of Geneva, the best of Lambeth
Aesthetically speaking
In its sumptuously sober
Interior, meet.

A continuous gallery, clear glass in the windows
An elegant conventicle
In the Ionian order—
What Dissenter with taste
But would turn, on these terms,
Episcopalian?

"Dissenter" and "tasteful" are contradictions
In terms, perhaps, and my fathers
Would ride again to the Boyne
Or with scythes to Sedgemoor, or splinter
The charming fanlights in this charming slum
By their lights, rightly.

Dissentient Voice

1. *A Baptist Childhood*

When some were happy as the grass was green,
I was as happy as a glass was dark,
Chill eye beneath the chapel floor unseen
Most of the year, a mystery, the Ark.

Aboveboard rose the largely ethical
Glossy-with-graining pulpit; underground
The older Scriptures trembled for the Fall
And lapped at Adam with a sucking sound.

Grass-rooted goodness and a joy unmixed
Parch unbaptized inside a droughty head;
Arcadia's floor is not so firmly fixed
But it must tremble to a pastor's tread.

2. *Dissent. A Fable.*

When Bradbury sang, "The Roast Beef of Old England"
And Watts, "How doth the little busy bee",
Then Doddridge blessed the pikes of Cumberland
And plunging sapphics damned eternally.

Said Watts the fox: "Your red meat is uncouth.
We'll keep the bleeding purchase out of sight.
Arminian honey for the age's tooth!
With so much sweetness, who will ask for light?"

Wolf Bradbury mauled the synod, but the fox
Declared that men were growing more refined;
And honey greased, where blood would rust, the locks
That clicked when Calvin trapped the open mind.

The wolves threw off sheeps' clothing once or twice

(For Queen Anne dead, or the Pretender foiled),
But the fox knew that tastes were growing nice
And unction kept the hinge of dogma oiled.

Foxes however are their own worst foes;
And now their chapel door stands open wide,
Its hinge so clogged with wax it cannot close,
No fish so queer but he can swim inside.

The queerest fishes hunger for the trap
And wish the door would close on them, the rough
Jaws of Geneva and Old England snap;
They think their church not barbarous enough.

The fable seems extravagant, no doubt.
But Reynard ruled the roosts of heaven then,
And beastly pastors kept true shepherds out
While pike and barracuda fished for men.

   3. *Portrait of the Artist as a Farmyard Fowl*
Pluming himself upon a sense of sin
      (Lice in his feathers' undersides)
He sported drab, the sooner Faith to win.
      Old zealots were such sobersides;
He felt their gooseflesh crawl upon his skin
      And hoped to feel their zeal besides.

Since then this would-be puritan has paced
      A cock unmatched although so spurred;
Purist who crowed at shadows, he debased
      The rate of evil and conferred
Its rights on squalor, out of sheer good taste.
      No hag would ride on such a bird.

Dark plumes, though puritanical in cut,
     Still clothe the cock of the studied walk;
A conscious carriage must become a strut;
     Fastidiousness can only stalk
And seem at last not even tasteful but
     A ruffled hen too apt to squawk.

4. *A Gathered Church.*
(In memoriam A.E.D. ob. 1939)
Deacon, you are to recognise in this
The idlest of my avocations, fruit
Of some late casual studies and my need
(Not dire, nor much acknowledged as a claim
Upon your known munificence) for what
You as lay preacher loved and disavowed,
The mellow tang of eloquence—a food
I have some skill in rendering down from words
Suppose them choice and well matured. I heard
Such from your bee-mouth once. A tarnished sun
Swirling the motes that swarmed along its shaft
Mixed soot with spices, and with honey, dust;
And memories of that winning unction now
Must countenance this application. For
I see them tumbled in a frowzy beam,
The grains of dust or pollen from our past
Our common stock in family and church,
Asking articulation. These affairs
Touched you no doubt more nearly; you are loath
To see them made a gaud of rhetoric. But, sir,
I will deal plainly with you. They are past,
Past hoping for as you had hoped for them

For sixty years or more the day you died,
And if I seem a fribble in this case
No matter. For I will be eloquent
And on these topics, having little choice.
You who were once an orator should know
How these things are decided, not by chance
Although to think so is our best recourse;
For we may pledge our faith that they are solved
In part by fervent feeling and in part
By strenuous intellection—so they are,
But by all these under the guise of chance,
Of happy yet exacting accident,
Out of whose bounty suddenly a word
Of no apparent pertinence or force
Will promise unaccountably to draw
The whole lax beam into a burning-glass.
So here I take the husk of my research,
A form of words—the phrase, "a gathered church",
A rallying cry of our communions once
For you perhaps still stirring, but for me
A picturesque locution, nothing more
Except for what it promises, a tang.
Here is the promise of the burning-glass;
Now turn it in the variegated light.

"A gathered church". That posy, the elect,
Was gathered in, not into, garden-walls;
For God must out of sheer caprice resect
The jugular stalks of those He culls and calls.

Watts thought his church, though scant of privilege,
Walled in its own communion. In its walks
Some may have doubted if so sparse a hedge
Tempered the blast to blooms still on their stalks.

It was the rooted flower could be hurt:
The plucked that lived in living water felt
No more the stress of time, the tug of dirt.
Time lost for good the fragrance Heaven smelt.

When blossoms crowd into the waist of time,
Those cut and chosen for the eternal vase
Rot down to no kind humus, rather climb
And spend their charity upon the stars.

Abundant friction: not a deal of heat.
These are, you know, preliminary rites,
A form of invocation. So the glass
Is moved and dances, waterish, flashes out
Now on the wall, now on the floor . . . But now
Your face swims up athwart the light,
The silken, heavy, iron-grey moustache
That reaffirms conciliatory smiles
Dispensing honey with a Dorset burr;
The hollow temples of a young man's brow;
The mild and beaming eye; the cheek still apple-hale.
Appealing gestures pregnantly curtailed
Conveyed impulsive courtesies, refined
The gross freak of your corpulence. That head
Was bowed beneath reproaches mostly mute
When "Charity begins at home", we said,
Feeling the pinch of your more public alms
Wise in our generations. And indeed

You thought so too; your home was somewhere else
And there you ran most fruitfully to seed.
Now all the churches gathered from the world
Through that most crucial bottleneck of Grace,
That more than hourglàss, being waspish, waist
Where all the flutes of love are gathered in,
The girdle of Eternity, the strait
Too straitened for the sands and sons of Time,
More mean and private than the sticking-place
Of any partial loyalties—all these
In you, dear sir, are justified. Largesse,
Suppose it but of rhetoric, endears,
Disseminated quite at large to bless
The waste, superb profusion of the spheres.

Gardens No Emblems

Man with a scythe: the torrent of his swing
Finds its own level; and is not hauled back
But gathers fluently, like water rising
Behind the watergates that close a lock.

The gardener eased his foot into a boot;
Which action like the mower's had its mould,
Being itself a sort of taking root,
Feeling for lodgment in the leather's fold.

But forms of thought move in another plane
Whose matrices no natural forms afford
Unless subjected to prodigious strain:
Say, light proceeding edgewise, like a sword.

Heigh-ho on a Winter Afternoon

There is a heigh-ho in these glowing coals
By which I sit wrapped in my overcoat
As if for a portrait by Whistler. And there is
A heigh-ho in the bird that noiselessly
Flew just now past my window, to alight
On winter's moulding, snow; and an alas,
A heigh-ho and a desultory chip,
Chip, chip on stone from somewhere down below.

Yes I have "mellowed", as you said I would,
And that's a heigh-ho too for any man;
Heigh-ho that means we fall short of alas
Which sprigs the grave of higher hopes than ours.
Yet heigh-ho too has its own luxuries,
And salts with courage to be jocular
Disreputable sweets of wistfulness,
By deprecation made presentable.

What should we do to rate the long alas
But skeeter down a steeper gradient?
And then some falls are still more fortunate,
The meteors spent, the tragic heroes stunned
Who go out like a light. But here the chip,
Chip, chip will flake the stone by slow degrees,
For hour on hour the fire will gutter down,
The bird will call at longer intervals.

Against Confidences

Loose lips now
Call Candour friend
Whom Candour's brow,
When clear, contemned.

Candour can live
Within no shade
That our compulsive
Needs have made

On couches where
We sleep, confess,
Couple and share
A pleased distress.

Not to dispense
With privacies,
But reticence
His practice is;

Agreeing where
Is no denial,
Not to spare
One truth from trial,

But to respect
Conviction's plight
In Intellect's
Hard equal light.

Not to permit,
To shy belief
Too bleakly lit,
The shade's relief

Clouds Candour's brow,
But to indulge
These mouths that now
Divulge, divulge.

Nineteen-Seventeen

A glass in a Liverpool drawing room cracked across.
A telegram fell out of it for Rica.
Perfidious glass that would not mirror loss,
The omen had outstripped the telegram.

A glass in Roscoe's drawing room fell apart
And handed out a telegram from France..
Rica got up from winding bandages.

The gaze of the glass was frantic and averted.
A wet and severed wrist, a hand that shook
Came from the mirror and delivered death
To Liverpool and England in a look.

She reckoned there could not be long to wait.
A wedge of wrack was hunting in from sea
As stadiums spill spectators from a gate.
The thrumming bolt approached her from the blue.
Its piercing note already shattered glass.

A world of plush and leather came to pieces,
Mahogany was shivered into glass.
She smiled farewell to all their startled faces
And steadily outstripped the telegram.

To a Brother in the Mystery

Circa 1290.

The world of God has turned its two stone faces
One my way, one yours. Yet we change places
A little, slowly. After we had halved
The work between us, those grotesques I carved
There in the first bays clockwise from the door,
That was such work as I got credit for
At York and Beverley: thorn-leaves twined and bent
To frame some small and human incident
Domestic or of venery. Each time I crossed
Since then, however, underneath the vast
Span of our Mansfield limestone, to appraise
How you cut stone, my emulous hard gaze
Has got to know you as I know the stone
Where none but chisels talk for us. I have grown
Of my own way of thinking yet of yours,
Seeing your leafage burgeon there by the doors
With a light that, flickering, trenches the voussoir's line;
Learning your pre-harmonies, design
Nourished by exuberance, and fine-drawn
Severity that is tenderness, I have thought,
Looking at these last stalls that I have wrought
This side of the chapter's octagon, I find
No hand but mine at work, yet mine refined
By yours, and all the difference: my motif
Of foliate form, your godliness in leaf.
    And your last spandrel proves the debt incurred
Not all on the one side. There I see a bird
Pecks at your grapes, and after him a fowler,
A boy with a bow. Elsewhere, your leaves discover
Of late blank mask-like faces. We infect

Each other then, doubtless to good effect . . .
And yet, take care: this cordial knack bereaves
The mind of all its sympathy with leaves,
Even with stone. I would not take away
From your peculiar mastery, if I say
A sort of coldness is the core of it,
A sort of cruelty; that prerequisite
Perhaps I rob you of, and in exchange give
What? Vulgarity's prerogative,
Indulgence towards the frailties it indulges,
Humour called "wryness" that acknowledges
Its own complicity. I can keep in mind
So much at all events, can always find
Fallen humanity enough, in stone,
Yes, in the medium; where we cannot own
Crispness, compactness, elegance, but the feature
Seals it and signs it work of human nature
And fallen though redeemable. You, I fear,
Will find you bought humanity too dear
At the price of some light leaves, if you begin
To find your handling of them growing thin,
Insensitive, brittle. For the common touch,
Though it warms, coarsens. Never care so much
For leaves or people, but you care for stone
A little more. The medium is its own
Thing, and not all a medium, but the stuff
Of mountains; cruel, obdurate, and rough.

Killala*

Forlorn indeed Hope on these shores,
White-breeched, under a tricorne, shouting orders
Into the wind in a European language
La gloire against the Atlantic.
                                                And Enniscrone,
The unfocussed village carefully grouped on absence . . .

Laden with Europe, toiling up out of the sea
With all the baggage of their own and Europe's
History barnacled, clammy with tawny jellies
And spotted silts, the wreck
Of unwashed hope is a more combustible flotsam
Than this more stranded,
More featureless than any conurbation.

Not memory (her lading) nor the vessel
—No, nor the vessel, for the *Téméraire*
Has been a dozen ships and all one venture—
But the venture persists. Such a temerity,
So bare a chance deserves a barer rock's
Less cluttered landfall. Nakedness
Is structural, asks a binnacle at sea;
By land, if not an oak, a standing stone
Hewn or unhewn in an open place, for the venture
To take a shape by. But the prudent Gael,
Disguised on the skyline as habitation tatters
A scarecrow coast, has blurred identity
By blurring shape, a flutter of rags in the wind.

Frenchman, the beacons flare across the Midlands.

* *Killala:* where the French landed in Ireland in 1798.

Stopping the car and hating this ugly place,
Let this be as if I had lit the first of the beacons,
Of driftwood fetched from the shore,
Announcing your identity and presence:
Not an idea, abstract notion, quality
But a being only, able for life and action,
The same it was some time ago, in France.

With the Grain

Why, by an ingrained habit, elevate
    Into their own ideas
Activities like carpentry, become
    The metaphors of graining?
Gardening, the one word, tilth? Or thought,
    The idea of having ideas,
Resolved into images of tilth and graining?

An ingrained habit . . . This is fanciful:
    And there's the rub
Bristling, where the irritable block
    Screams underneath the blade
Of love's demand, or in crimped and gouged-out
    Shavings only, looses
Under a peeling logic its perceptions.

Language (mine, when wounding,
    Yours, back-biting) lacks
No whorl nor one-way shelving. It resists,
    Screams its remonstrance, planes
Reluctantly to a level. And the most
    Reasonable of settlements betrays
Unsmoothed resentment under the caress.

2.

The purest hue, let only the light be sufficient,
    Turns colour. And I was told
If painters frequent St. Ives
    It is because the light
There, under the cliff, is merciful. I dream

Of an equable light upon words
And as painters paint in St. Ives, the poets speaking.

Under that cliff we should say, my dear,
    Not what we mean, but what
The words would mean. We should speak,
    As carpenters work,
With the grain of our words. We should utter
    Unceasingly the hue of love
Safe from the battery of changeable light.

(Love, a condition of such fixed colour,
    Cornwall indeed, or Wales
Might foster. Lovers in mauve,
    Like white-robed Druids
Or the Bards in blue, would need
    A magical philtre, no less,
Like Iseult's, to change partners.)

3.

Such a fourth estate of the realm,
    Hieratic unwinking
Mauve or blue under skies steel-silver,
    Would chamfer away
A knot in the grain of a streaming light, the glitter,
    Off lances' points, that moved
A sluggish Froissart to aesthetic feeling.

And will the poet, carpenter of light,
    Work with the grain henceforward?
If glitterings won't fetch him
    Nor the refractory crystal,
Will he never again look into the source of light

Aquiline, but fly
Always out of the sun, unseen till softly alighting?

Why, by an ingrained habit, elevate
    Into the light of ideas
The colourful trades, if not like Icarus
    To climb the beam? High lights
Are always white, but this ideal sun
    Dyes only more intensely, and we find
Enough cross-graining in the most abstract nature.

Red Rock of Utah

> of golde and sylver they make com-
> monly chaumber pottes, and other
> vesselles, that serve for moste vile
> uses. . . . Furthermore of the same
> mettalles they make greate chaines,
> fetters, and gieves wherin they tie
> their bondmen. Finally whosoever
> for anye offense be infamed, by their
> eares hang rynges of golde, upon
> their fyngers they weare rynges of
> golde, and aboute their neckes
> chaines of golde, and in conclusion
> their heades be tied aboute with
> gold.
>
> —More's *Utopia.*

Surely it has some virtue, having none,
Sighed to her bondman the Utopian lady
Telling the links of gold among his hair.
At wrist and ankle, fingers, head and neck
The unserviceable metal he must wear
In rings, chains, chainmail bonnets, riveted
Locked, knotted, wound on him whom her affection
Chose she conceived perversely; till she guessed
Its virtue was in helmeting that head,
A collar round the neck she hung upon.

What colour were Utopia's rocks?
Navajo red, the Mormon wives
Mutter, restless in drab smocks,
Would void the golden chamberpots
And strike off the golden gyves
In crimson Zion. Under the mesa's
Coronet, taken from such base uses,
Shall not red gold deck the wives of Utah?

"Convicting us, convict the Lord
Of barbarous inutilities:
What left His hand but a very gaud,
Red over canyon and mesa, good
For nothing but an artifice
To adorn His favoured? Little we ask
Who wintered for Him in Nebraska:
Red gold only, a little at wrist or ankle."

"Has it then every virtue, having none?"
Sighs to the Lord in prayer the Mormon lady
And Nephi Johnson remonstrates, "What good
The land, if not for cotton?" But the Lord,
Dear reverend pioneers, in His red blood
Sealed more than that hard promise of a sod
To turn in Zion. Planting such dubious
Capacities in your sons as might applaud
Gauds of gratuitous ornament in your God,
Your God depraved King Utopus himself.

Reflections on Deafness

For Kenneth and Margaret Millar

1.

Making the best and most of a visitation,
The deaf can make it serve their purposes.
What else can any one use but his condition?
Is affliction turned to use the less affliction?

2.

The voice called ours, played back to us on tape,
We hate at once, disown. The nerve of selfhood
Jumps at the drill of an achieved imposture.
The deaf cannot tell the King from the Pretender.

3.

The blind have rights in that most delicate
And intimate of the senses, touch; the deaf
Lip-reader, in somnambulistic rape
On the act of sight, usurps the rights denied him.

Blindness that can be rectified by reason,
Errors of calculation not in will
We tolerate; but wince to see the human,
Distinguishingly human act of speech contorted.

4.

Yes, we are deaf to their condition, hear
All that we want to hear, the blind man's stick
Redeemably tap-tapping, but the voice
That cannot hear itself we cannot hear.

For an Age of Plastics

With the effect almost of carving the hillside
    They climb in their stiff terraces, these houses
Feed the returning eye with national pride
    In the "built to last." Approving elegance
Where there is only decency, the eye
    Applauds the air of nothing left to chance
Or brilliantly provisional. Not the fact
    But the air of it, the illusion, we observe;
Chance in the bomb sight kept these streets intact
    And razed whole districts. Nor was the lesson lost
On the rebuilt Plymouth, how an age of chance
    Is an age of plastics. In a style pre-cast
Pre-fabricated, and as if its site
    Were the canyon's lip, it rises out of rubble
Sketchily massive, moulded in bakelite.

Annoyed to take a gloomy sort of pride
    In numbering our losses, I suppose
The ploughman ceased his carving of the hillside
    And all the coulters and the chisels broke
When he was young whom we come home to bury,
    A man like clay in the hands of his womenfolk.

A ploughman carved three harvests, each a son,
    Upon the flesh of Wales. And all were carried
Long since from those hillsides, yet this one
    Comes first to threshing. Nutriment and grain
For all the mashing of the interim
    Live in the load of him. Living again
His shipwright's years, the countryman's walks in the park,
    The scrape of a mattock in a too small garden,
The marriage to the capable matriarch,

What would he change? Perhaps a stubbornness
That bristled sometimes, for the sensible hands
    To circumvent and gentle, would be less
Amenable to their shaping. But all told,
    His edged tools still would lie in the garden shed,
Still he would flow, himself, from mould to mould.

Whatever he showed of something in the rough,
    Sluggish in flow and unadaptable,
I liked him for; affecting to be gruff,
    An awkward customer—so much was due,
He seemed to think, to what a man was, once:
    Something to build with, take a chisel to.

The Life of Service

Service, or Latin *sorbus,* European
More especially English shadbush or small tree,
Asks all the shade the fancier can find
In a walled garden. This is no plebeian
Of cottage plots, though coarse in leaf and rind.

Planted, it is persistent, of a thick
Skin, and grows strong the more it's trodden on;
Or afterwards, as an established upas,
Thrives all the better by each welcomed nick
Of aggrieved knives wielded by interlopers.

By this indeed it knows itself. Self-thwarted,
It welcomes parasites, for playing host
To what insults and saps it is its virtue
And its fulfilment. Flourishing contorted,
All its long-suffering's overbearing too.

Some cultivators hold that it repays,
By its small edible fruit (in favoured species
Of a vinous taste), its culture. It does not;
All saner growth abhors it, and the Bays
Wither, affronted, in the poisoned plot.

The 'Sculpture' of Rhyme

Potter nor iron-founder
Nor caster of bronze will he cherish,
But the monumental mason;

As if his higher stake
Than the impregnable spiders
Of self-defended music

Procured him mandibles
To chisel honey from the saxifrage,
And a mouth to graze on feldspar.